THE ILLUSTRATED

Emily Dickinson

25 ESSENTIAL POEMS

EDITED BY
RYAN G.
VAN CLEAVE

BUSHEL
& PECK
BOOKS

BUSHEL
& PECK
BOOKS

Published by Bushel & Peck Books, www.bushelandpeckbooks.com.

Bushel & Peck Books is dedicated to fighting illiteracy all over the world.
For every book we sell, we donate one to a child in need——book for book.
To nominate a school or organization to receive free books,
please visit www.bushelandpeckbooks.com.

Design and illustration by David Miles.
Type set in Baskerville and Calder.
Collage illustrations were created digitally from various public domain works
and/or elements licensed from Shutterstock.com.

LCCN: TK
ISBN: 9781638191070

First Edition

Printed in China

10 9 8 7 6 5 4 3

Selections

THE NATURAL WORLD

A Bird came down the Walk – 6

A Light exists in Spring 8

I started Early – Took my Dog – 10

The Grass so little has to do – 12

Make me a picture of the sun – 14

She sweeps with many-colored Brooms – 17

I robbed the Woods – 19

A narrow Fellow in the Grass 20

A Drop fell on the Apple Tree – 22

IDEAS & IMAGINATION

He ate and drank the precious Words – 27

I felt a Funeral, in my Brain, ... 29

Success is counted sweetest 30

"Hope" is the thing with feathers – 33

Because I could not stop for Death – 34

Tell all the Truth but tell it slant – 37

I'm Nobody! Who are you? 39

I dwell in Possibility – 41

A Thought went up my mind today – 43

HEART & SPIRIT

I never saw a Moor – 46

The Murmur of a Bee 49

If I can stop one Heart from breaking 51

These are the days when Birds come back – 52

There's a certain Slant of light, ... 55

God gave a Loaf to every Bird – 57

The Daisy follows soft the Sun – 59

INTRODUCTION

Welcome to the Illustrated Poets Collection! Here are three suggestions to help you make the most of this book.

SUGGESTION 1: Enjoy the poems. This seems far more important than trying to puzzle out what the author meant (or what other people believe the author meant).

SUGGESTION 2: Engage with the poems by asking questions. Here are three that should prove useful for any poem you encounter:

- *What do you notice about this poem?*

- *How does this poem make you feel?*

- *What else have you read/seen/experienced that connects with this poem?*

You'll also find individual questions suggested for each poem in this book.

SUGGESTION 3: Be your own boss. Read the poems in order or jump around as you see fit. Share them or savor them all by yourself. Say them aloud or whisper their words in your heart.

Poetry makes life better. There is NO wrong way to experience a poem.

So, read on, dear friend. And thank you for choosing poetry.

Ryan G. Van Cleave
Series Editor

PART I

The Natural World

A BIRD CAME DOWN
THE WALK –

A Bird came down the Walk –
He did not know I saw –
He bit an Angleworm in halves
And ate the fellow, raw.

And then he drank a Dew
From a convenient Grass –
And then hopped sidewise to the Wall
To let a Beetle pass –

He glanced with rapid eyes
That hurried all abroad –
They looked like frightened Beads, I thought –
He stirred his Velvet Head

Like one in danger, Cautious,
I offered him a Crumb
And he unrolled his feathers
And rowed him softer Home –

Than Oars divide the Ocean,
Too silver for a **seam** –
Or Butterflies, off Banks of Noon,
Leap, **plashless**, as they swim.

Than Oars divide the O
Too silver for a seam
Or Butterflies, off B
Leap, plashless, as the.
m softer H

⚙ **ENGAGE**

What do you think the speaker is feeling when spying on the bird at the start of the poem?

At what point does the bird become aware of the watcher?

Who/what is swimming at the end of the poem?

💡 **IMAGINE**

How would the story of this poem be different if it were told from the bird's point of view?

🔤 **DEFINE**

seam: *ripple of water*

plashless: *without a splash*

A LIGHT EXISTS
IN SPRING

A Light exists in Spring
Not present on the Year
At any other period –
When March is scarcely here

A Color stands abroad
On Solitary Fields
That Science cannot overtake
But Human Nature feels.

It waits upon the Lawn,
It shows the furthest Tree
Upon the furthest Slope you know
It almost speaks to you.

Then, as Horizons step
Or Noons report away
Without the Formula of sound,
It passes and we stay –

A quality of loss
Affecting our Content
As Trade had suddenly **encroached**
Upon a **Sacrament**.

ENGAGE

Where do you see instances of personification (giving human attributes to something)?

Why include scientific and religious references in a poem about nature?

What else is lost when the light goes away?

IMAGINE

If this poem were edible, what would it taste like?

DEFINE

encroached:
intruded upon

Sacrament:
religious ceremony

I STARTED EARLY –
TOOK MY DOG –

I started Early – Took my Dog –
And visited the Sea –
The Mermaids in the Basement
Came out to look at me,

And **Frigates** – in the Upper Floor
Extended **Hempen** Hands –
Presuming Me to be a Mouse –
Aground – upon the Sands –

But no Man moved Me – till the Tide
Went past my simple Shoe –
And past my Apron – and my Belt
And past my **Bodice** – too –

And made as He would eat me up –
As wholly as a Dew
Upon a Dandelion's Sleeve –
And then – I started – too –

And He – He followed – close behind –
I felt His Silver Heel
Upon my Ankle – Then My Shoes
Would overflow with Pearl –

Until We met the Solid Town –
No One He seemed to know –
And bowing – with a Mighty look –
At me – That Sea withdrew –

Who do you imagine the speaker is in this poem?

In what way does this particular walk with a dog become extraordinary?

What moments in the poem seem threatening?

IMAGINE

If you were going to make a short movie based on this poem, whom would you cast as the main character?

Would their companion be a dog, another animal, or even a person?

DEFINE

Frigates: *large ships*

Hempen: *rough fabric made from hemp plants*

Bodice: *tight-fitting upper part of a dress*

THE GRASS SO
LITTLE HAS TO DO –

The Grass so little has to do –
A Sphere of simple Green –
With only Butterflies to brood
And Bees to entertain –

And stir all day to pretty Tunes
The Breezes fetch along –
And hold the Sunshine in its lap
And bow to everything –

And thread the Dews, all night, like Pearls –
And make itself so fine
A **Duchess** were too common
For such noticing –

And even when it dies – to pass
In Odors so divine –
Like Lowly spices, lain to sleep –
Or **Spikenards**, perishing –

And then, in **Sovereign** Barns to dwell –
And dream the Days away,
The Grass so little has to do,
I wish I were a Hay –

The first line suggests the life of grass is simple and boring. Does the rest of the poem support that idea?

Does time seem to move slowly or quickly in this poem?

Why might someone wish to be dead grass (hay) instead of live grass?

IMAGINE

If grass were a person, what type of person would it be?

Do you know anybody like that?

Would you want to be friends with them?

DEFINE

Duchess: *wife of a duke (a high rank of nobility)*

Spikenards: *fragrant Asian flower used in perfume*

Sovereign: *having ultimate power*

MAKE ME A PICTURE OF THE SUN –

Make me a picture of the sun –
So I can hang it in my room –
And make believe I'm getting warm
When others call it "Day"!

Draw me a Robin – on a stem –
So I am hearing him, I'll dream,
And when the Orchards stop their tune –
Put my **pretense** – away –

Say if it's really – warm at noon –
Whether it's **Buttercups** – that "skim" –
Or Butterflies – that "bloom"?
Then – skip – the frost – upon the **lea** –
And skip the **Russet** – on the tree –
Let's play those – never come!

ENGAGE

Does this speaker see make believe, dreams, and play as a positive thing?

Why might a robin be on a stem instead of a branch?

How seriously do you take the last line?

IMAGINE

Give this poem a theme song. What are your favorite options?

DEFINE

pretense: *false appearance*

Buttercups: *plant with yellow cup-shaped flowers*

lea: *pasture*

Russet: *reddish-brown color*

SHE SWEEPS WITH MANY-COLORED BROOMS –

She sweeps with many-colored Brooms –
And leaves the Shreds behind –
Oh Housewife in the Evening West –
Come back, and dust the Pond!

You dropped a Purple **Ravelling** in,
You dropped an **Amber** thread –
And now you've littered all the East
With **Duds** of Emerald!

And still, she **plies** her spotted Brooms,
And still the Aprons fly,
Till Brooms fade softly into stars –
And then I come away –

ENGAGE

Is the "She" an actual housewife?

How do the repeated words and phrases affect the poem?

Do you think Emily Dickinson is the "I" in the final line?

IMAGINE

What single word is the most important one in this poem?

If that word were removed or changed, how would this poem read differently?

DEFINE

Ravelling: *woven fiber*

Amber: *yellow color of fossilized tree sap*

Duds: *clothing*

plies: *uses*

I ROBBED THE WOODS –

I robbed the Woods –
The trusting Woods.
The unsuspecting Trees
Brought out their **Burs** and mosses
My fantasy to please.
I scanned their **trinkets** curious –
I grasped – I bore away –
What will the solemn **Hemlock** –
What will the Oak tree say?

ENGAGE

Are the trees putting their decorations ("Burs and mosses") on display to be considered and taken?

What do you imagine the trees in this poem will say?

Is this a serious or playful poem?

IMAGINE

Think about someone you admire. What would they like most about this poem?

What would they say about it?

DEFINE

Burs: *seed containers with hooks that catch on animal fur*

trinkets: *items of little value*

Hemlock: *evergreen tree*

A NARROW FELLOW
IN THE GRASS

A narrow Fellow in the Grass
Occasionally rides –
You may have met Him – did you not
His notice sudden is –

The Grass divides as with a Comb –
A spotted shaft is seen –
And then it closes at your Feet
And opens further on –

He likes a **Boggy** Acre
A Floor too cool for Corn –
Yet when a Boy, and Barefoot –
I more than once at Noon

Have passed, I thought, a Whip Lash
Unbraiding in the Sun
When stooping to secure it,
It wrinkled, and was gone –

Several of Nature's People
I know, and they know me –
I feel for them a **transport**
Of **cordiality** –

But met this Fellow
Attended, or alone
Without a tighter Breathing
And Zero at the Bone –

*How does the speaker
feel about nature in
general? About the
snake?*

*Do those feelings change
throughout the poem?*

*Which description
in the poem is your
favorite?*

IMAGINE

*This poem thinks it's a
know-it-all. What does
it think it knows?*

*Why does it think it's
so smart?*

DEFINE

Boggy: *wet and
muddy*

transport: *thrill*

cordiality:
friendliness

21

A DROP FELL ON
THE APPLE TREE –

A Drop fell on the Apple Tree –
Another – on the Roof –
A Half a Dozen kissed the **Eaves** –
And made the **Gables** laugh –

A few went out to help the Brook
That went to help the Sea –
Myself **Conjectured** were they Pearls –
What Necklaces could be –

The Dust replaced, in **Hoisted** Roads –
The Birds **jocoser** sung –
The Sunshine threw his Hat away –
The Bushes – spangles flung –

The Breezes brought dejected **Lutes** –
And bathed them in the Glee –
The Orient put out a single Flag,
And signed the **Fete** away.

ENGAGE

How welcome is this summer rain shower?

What are some of the more unexpected word choices in this poem?

Which of the stanzas best captures the experience of a summer storm?

IMAGINE

Draw the map of this poem. Include all the relevant sites, stops, and secrets.

DEFINE

Eaves: *overhanging part of a roof*

Gables: *triangular part that holds up a peaked roof*

Conjectured: *imagined*

Hoisted: *raised*

jocoser: *playfully*

Lutes: *small stringed instruments*

Fcte: *celebration*

PART II

Ideas & Imagination

HE ATE AND DRANK THE PRECIOUS WORDS –

He ate and drank the precious Words –
His Spirit grew **robust** –
He knew no more that he was poor,
Nor that his **frame** was Dust –

He danced along the dingy Days,
And this **Bequest** of Wings
Was but a Book – What **Liberty**
A loosened spirit brings –

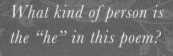

ENGAGE

What kind of person is the "he" in this poem?

What "Bequest of Wings" might a book offer?

What's the last book that you "ate and drank"?

IMAGINE

Do you know someone who would enjoy this poem? Share it with them.

DEFINE

robust: *strong, healthy*

frame: *body*

Bequest: *inheritance*

Liberty: *freedom*

I FELT A FUNERAL,
IN MY BRAIN,

I felt a Funeral, in my Brain,
And Mourners, to and fro,
Kept treading – **treading** – till it seemed
That Sense was breaking through –

And when they all were seated,
A Service, like a Drum –
Kept beating – beating – till I thought
My Mind was going numb –

And then I heard them lift a Box
And creak across my Soul
With those same Boots of Lead, again,
Then Space – began to toll

As all the Heavens were a Bell,
And Being, but an ear,
And I, and Silence, some strange Race,
Wrecked, solitary, here –

And then a Plank in Reason, broke,
And I dropped down, and down –
And hit a World, at every plunge,
And Finished knowing – then –

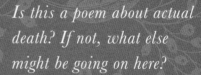

ENGAGE

Is this a poem about actual death? If not, what else might be going on here?

What's the relationship between the speaker and silence (that "strange race") at the end?

How do you make sense of a poem that ends with an unfinished sentence or thought?

IMAGINE

Set a timer, then see how long it takes you to go back through the poem to find three specific things you didn't notice before (like an interesting image, a surprising line break, or an unusual capitalization).

Challenge a friend to do the same thing, and see who can locate new things faster.

DEFINE

treading: *walking*

SUCCESS IS COUNTED SWEETEST

Success is counted sweetest
By those who **ne'er** succeed.
To comprehend a nectar
Requires **sorest** need.

Not one of all the **purple Host**
Who **took the Flag** today
Can tell the definition
So clear of Victory

As he defeated – dying –
On whose forbidden ear
The distant strains of triumph
Burst agonized and clear!

⚙ ENGAGE

Are "those who ne'er succeed" truly most able to appreciate success?

Which is more powerful— the longing for success or the satisfaction of having success?

What are some of your favorite examples of success?

⚡ IMAGINE

Choose one of your examples of success and create a four- line stanza modeled after any of those in this poem.

🔤 DEFINE

ne'er: *never*

sorest: *aching*

purple Host: *army*

took the Flag: *win a battle*

"HOPE" IS THE THING WITH FEATHERS –

"Hope" is the thing with feathers –
That perches in the soul –
And sings the tune without the words –
And never stops – at all –

And sweetest – in the **Gale** – is heard –
And sore must be the storm –
That could **abash** the little Bird
That kept so many warm –

I've heard it in the chillest land –
And on the strangest Sea –
Yet, never, in **Extremity**,
It asked a crumb – of Me.

ENGAGE

What do you think of when you think about Hope?

How does the poem connect a bird and Hope?

Why doesn't Hope ask "a crumb – of Me"?

IMAGINE

How would you act out this poem if you were asked to perform it?

Would you be yourself, a bird, or some other type of animal?

DEFINE

Gale: *strong wind*

abash: *overwhelm*

Extremity: *great difficulty*

Because I could not stop for Death –
He kindly stopped for me –
The Carriage held but just Ourselves –
And Immortality.

We slowly drove – He knew no haste
And I had put away
My labor and my leisure too,
For His **Civility** –

We passed the School, where Children strove
At Recess – in the Ring –
We passed the Fields of Gazing Grain –
We passed the Setting Sun –

Or rather – He passed Us –
The Dews drew quivering and chill –
For only **Gossamer**, my Gown –
My **Tippet** – only **Tulle** –

We paused before a House that seemed
A Swelling of the Ground –
The Roof was scarcely visible –
The **Cornice** – in the Ground –

Since then – 'tis Centuries – and yet
Feels shorter than the Day
I first **surmised** the Horses' Heads
Were toward Eternity –

ENGAGE

This poem doesn't use emotional language. Why not?

What do you imagine this speaker is feeling and thinking?

Where does the poem become darker and more unsettling?

IMAGINE

If you could ask this poem's speaker three questions, what would you ask? What do you imagine the answers might be?

DEFINE

Civility: *politeness*

Gossamer: *fine and delicate*

Tippet: *long scarf*

Tulle: *stiff, net-like fabric*

Cornice: *corner of a roof*

surmised: *guessed*

TELL ALL THE TRUTH BUT TELL IT SLANT –

Tell all the Truth but tell it slant –
Success in **Circuit** lies
Too bright for our **infirm** Delight
The Truth's superb surprise
As Lightning to the Children eased
With explanation kind
The Truth must dazzle gradually
Or every man be blind –

ENGAGE

In what ways might "Truth" be like lightning?

If the last line isn't about actual blindness, what might the poem be suggesting?

How might the "Truth" in the poem relate to poetry?

IMAGINE

Read this poem in a very public place. Then read it in a private place. How did the setting affect how you read the poem?

Did the poem's meaning change in those different settings?

DEFINE

Circuit: *circular route*

infirm: *weak*

I'M NOBODY! WHO ARE YOU?

I'm Nobody! Who are you?
Are you – Nobody – Too?
Then there's a pair of us!
Don't tell! they'd advertise – you know!

How dreary – to be – Somebody!
How public – like a Frog –
To tell one's name – the **livelong** June –
To an admiring **Bog**!

ENGAGE

What do you think it means to be a Nobody? Is that the same thing as what the speaker means here?

Why would being a Somebody be "dreary"?

Why do you think the speaker mentions a frog rather than another animal?

IMAGINE

Make three statements about this poem using the words "should," "would," and "could."

DEFINE

livelong: *entire*

Bog: *wet, muddy ground*

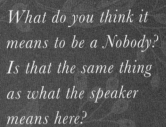

I DWELL IN POSSIBILITY –

I **dwell** in Possibility –
A fairer House than Prose –
More numerous of Windows –
Superior – for Doors –

Of Chambers as the Cedars –
Impregnable of Eye –
And for an Everlasting Roof
The **Gambrels** of the Sky –

Of Visitors – the fairest –
For Occupation – This –
The spreading wide my narrow Hands
To gather Paradise –

ENGAGE

How does poetry represent the idea of "Possibility"?

Why would a poetry house have an "Everlasting Roof" or more "Windows" than prose?

What kind of visitors would the speaker most want to see?

IMAGINE

Create a portrait of this poem. Invite a friend or family member to try this, too, and then compare your artwork.

DEFINE

dwell: *live*

Impregnable: *impossible to enter by force*

Gambrels: *roofs with two differently sloped sides*

*Have you ever "met" a
thought that you later
couldn't recall? How
did that make you feel?*

*What is the "Art" the
speaker refers to in the
middle stanza?*

*How does the speaker
feel about their lost
thought?*

*Write the bumper
sticker or fortune cookie
version of this poem.
Think short!*

A THOUGHT WENT UP
MY MIND TODAY –

A Thought went up my mind today –
That I have had before –
But did not finish – some way back –
I could not fix the Year –

Nor where it went – nor why it came
The second time to me –
Nor definitely, what it was –
Have I the Art to say –

But somewhere – in my Soul – I know –
I've met the Thing before –
It just reminded me – 'twas all –
And came my way no more –

PART III

Heart & Spirit

I NEVER SAW A
MOOR –

I never saw a **Moor** –
I never saw the Sea –
Yet know I how the **Heather** looks
And what a **Billow** be.

I never spoke with God
Nor visited in Heaven;
Yet certain am I of the spot
As if the **Checks** were given.

ENGAGE

Is this a hopeful poem?

If not, what emotion do you feel here?

If this poem needed a new title, what would you suggest?

IMAGINE

What have you never seen?

Create your own "I never saw a _____" four-line stanza. Bonus points for writing an entire poem!

DEFINE

Moor: *marshland*

Heather: *purple plant often found in moors*

Billow: *swell of waves or clouds*

Checks: *railroad tickets*

THE MURMUR OF A BEE

The Murmur of a Bee
A Witchcraft – **yieldeth** me –
If any ask me why –
'Twere easier to die –
Than tell –

The Red upon the Hill
Taketh away my will –
If anybody sneer –
Take care – for God is here –
That's all.

The Breaking of the Day
Addeth to my **Degree** –
If any ask me how –
Artist – who drew me so –
Must tell!

ENGAGE

In what ways might the "Murmur of a Bee" be "Witchcraft"?

What effect do the short lines create?

Who is the "Artist" who "drew me so"?

IMAGINE

Assume this poem is an advertisement. What's it trying to sell?

Are you buying?

DEFINE

yieldeth: *rewarded*

'Twere: *it were*

Degree: *relative intensity*

IF I CAN STOP ONE HEART FROM BREAKING

If I can stop one Heart from breaking
I shall not live in vain
If I can ease one Life the Aching
Or cool one Pain

Or help one fainting Robin
Unto his Nest again
I shall not live **in Vain**.

ENGAGE

Which heart does the speaker want to stop from breaking?

Why do you think the poet chose "Robin" instead of "bird"?

There's one small variation between the two repeated lines. What is it? What do you make of it?

IMAGINE

If this poem were a toy sold in a store, what would its packaging look like?

What would it say on the box?

What features would it promote?

DEFINE

in Vain: *to no purpose*

THESE ARE THE DAYS WHEN BIRDS COME BACK –

These are the days when Birds come back –
A very few – a Bird or two –
To take a backward look.

These are the days when skies resume
The old – old **sophistries** of June –
A blue and gold mistake.

Oh fraud that cannot cheat the Bee –
Almost thy **plausibility**
Induces my belief.

Till ranks of seeds their witness bear –
And softly thro' the altered air
Hurries a timid leaf.

Oh **Sacrament** of summer days,
Oh Last **Communion** in the Haze –
Permit a child to join.

Thy sacred **emblems** to partake –
Thy **consecrated** bread to break
And thine immortal wine!

⚙ ENGAGE

Why might only "a Bird or two" return "To take a backward look"?

What could they be looking at/for?

Why might that leaf be "timid"?

💡 IMAGINE

What do you think happened the day before the birds came back? What will happen the day after they leave?

📖 DEFINE

sophistries: *deceitful arguments*

plausibility: *reasonableness*

Induces: *leads to*

Sacrament: *religious ceremony*

Communion: *Christian ritual*

emblems: *symbolic objects*

consecrated: *made holy*

THERE'S A CERTAIN SLANT OF LIGHT,

There's a certain Slant of light,
Winter Afternoons –
That oppresses, like the **Heft**
Of **Cathedral** Tunes –

Heavenly Hurt, it gives us –
We can find no scar,
But internal difference,
Where the Meanings, are –

None may teach it – Any –
'Tis the **Seal** Despair –
An imperial **affliction**
Sent us of the Air –

When it comes, the Landscape listens –
Shadows – hold their breath –
When it goes, 'tis like the Distance
On the look of Death –

GOD GAVE A LOAF TO EVERY BIRD –

God gave a Loaf to every Bird –
But just a Crumb – to Me –
I dare not eat it – tho' I starve –
My **poignant** luxury –

To own it – touch it –
Prove the feat – that made the Pellet mine –
Too happy – for my **Sparrow**'s chance –
For Ampler **Coveting** –

It might be Famine – all around –
I could not miss an Ear –
Such Plenty smiles upon my **Board** –
My **Garner** shows so fair –

I wonder how the Rich – may feel –
An Indiaman – An Earl?
I deem that I – with but a Crumb –
Am **Sovereign** of them all –

THE DAISY FOLLOWS
SOFT THE SUN –

The Daisy follows soft the Sun –
And when his golden walk is done –
Sits shyly at his feet –
He – waking – finds the flower there –
Wherefore – **Marauder** – art thou here?
Because, Sir, love is sweet!

We are the Flower – Thou the Sun!
Forgive us, if as days decline –
We nearer **steal** to Thee!
Enamoured of the parting West –
The peace – the flight – the **Amethyst** –
Night's possibility!

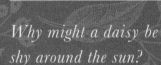
Why might a daisy be shy around the sun?

What do you make of old-fashioned language such as "Thou" and "Thee"?

What word or phrase are you most drawn to in this poem?

IMAGINE

Write the story of this poem…in exactly six words.

DEFINE

Marauder: *intruder*

steal: *move quietly*

Enamoured: *fascinated*

Amethyst: *purple precious stone*

Ten Things to Know About Emily Dickinson

1. Emily Elizabeth Dickinson (1830-1886) grew up in a prominent Amherst, Massachusetts, family and lived a very privileged life.

2. She went to Amherst Academy for seven years and briefly attended Mount Holyoke Female Seminary, so she had a solid classical education.

3. She never married, never had children, and rarely left the house to see friends. Toward the end of her life, she mostly stayed in her bedroom.

4. Her bedroom window looked out onto a cemetery, so she witnessed many funerals over the years.

5. She grew up in a time and place where Protestant Christianity was the norm, though her own religious beliefs were far less clear than those of her peers.

6. She loved gardening. She ran the family's greenhouse and grew hundreds of flowers, planted lots of vegetables, and tended to many apple, cherry, and pear trees.

7. She wrote nearly 1,800 poems, but fewer than a dozen got published while she was alive, and none of those included her name on them.

8. She was a prolific letter writer. She mailed thousands of letters to her friends, and occasionally she'd tuck a poem inside.

9. She rarely titled her poems, and she used unconventional capitalization as well as horizontal and vertical dashes.

10. Because she was influenced by hymns and ballads, many of her poems can be sung to the tune of "Amazing Grace," "The Yellow Rose of Texas," or the theme song of the TV show *Gilligan's Island.*

Commentary on the Poems

PART 1: THE NATURAL WORLD

"A Bird came down the Walk – "
The speaker secretly watches a robin gobble up lunch before it becomes frightened—perhaps by noticing the presence of the watcher. Offering a crumb sends the robin fleeing.

NOTICE THE CURIOUS REVERSAL WHERE THE SKY BECOMES SEA AND THE BIRD SWIMS OFF.

"A Light exists in Spring"
This nature poem marvels at the special quality of light in springtime.

NOTICE HOW THE ENDING SUGGESTS HOW MUCH OF A LOSS THERE IS WHEN THAT AMAZING LIGHT FINALLY VANISHES.

"I started Early – Took my Dog – "
A walk to the beach becomes magical and fantastic. The personified ocean appears to have feelings toward the speaker.

NOTICE WHERE THE SPEAKER GETS SCARED AND RETREATS FROM THE WATER.

"The Grass so little has to do – "
This dreamy nature poem explores the life and purpose of grass, metaphorically comparing it to a woman who makes a powerful duchess seem common.

NOTICE THE AMUSING END THAT MIGHT BE AN IDEALISTIC LOOK AT DEATH AND THE AFTERLIFE.

"Make me a picture of the sun – "
This speaker—probably a shut-in like Emily herself—asks for pictures of the natural world and seems content to remain in the world of imagination and make-believe.

NOTICE "PLAY" VERSUS THE EXPECTED "PRAY" IN THE FINAL LINE, WHICH KEEPS THINGS FROM GETTING TOO SERIOUS!

"She sweeps with many-colored Brooms – "
This poem shares how a beautiful sunset is created by a housewife sweeping.

NOTICE HOW THE POEM SHEDS SOME GLORIOUS LIGHT ON THE IMPRESSIVE WORK THAT HOMEMAKERS DO EVERY SINGLE DAY.

"I robbed the Woods – "
Emily and her younger sister often walked in the woods and brought back plants for her garden. This poem explores what the woods itself—personified, of course—thought about that.

NOTICE HOW THE BEGINNING OF THE POEM SEEMS HARSH ("ROBBED"), BUT THE ENDING IS MUCH MORE GENTLE.

"A narrow Fellow in the Grass"
A snake is seen in very human terms (calling the snake a "fellow"), which makes it seem less menacing than it otherwise might be.

NOTICE HOW THE "TIGHTER BREATHING" AT THE POEM'S END SPEAKS TO ANXIETY OR FEAR.

"A Drop fell on the Apple Tree – "
In vivid language, this poem shows how a few drops gradually become a rainstorm.

NOTICE HOW PERSONIFICATION MAKES THIS SCENE COME ALIVE IN MEMORABLE WAYS, AND THE ENDING SHOWS HOW THE WORLD IS BETTER AFTER THE STORM.

PART 2: IDEAS & IMAGINATION

"He ate and drank the precious Words – "
This poem reveals how an old man ("his frame was Dust") has found freedom ("Liberty") through reading.

NOTICE HOW BOOKS HELP HIM RE-EXPERIENCE LIFE IN POWERFUL WAYS.

"I felt a Funeral, in my Brain,"
A mental breakdown or perhaps even a literal death is presented as a funeral service. The ending is especially dark since the speaker ends up metaphorically shipwrecked within themselves, numb and alone among crushing silence.

NOTICE HOW THE LAST LINE STOPS JUST SHORT OF AN "AHA!" MOMENT, WHICH CAN'T HAPPEN WHEN ONE FALLS AWAY FROM "REASON."

"Success is counted sweetest"
This poem suggests that those who don't yet know victory are best suited to appreciate it.

NOTICE HOW THE CENTRAL IDEA OF THIS POEM IS RELEVANT BEYOND BATTLES AND WAR.

"'Hope' is the thing with feathers – "
This poem praises hope, which is metaphorically presented as a bird living within humans.

NOTICE HOW NO MATTER WHAT CHALLENGES ARE FACED (IN A "GALE" OR "THE CHILLEST LAND"), THE BIRD HAPPILY CHIRPS AWAY.

"Because I could not stop for Death – "
Here, Death seems gentlemanly ("kindly stopped" and "slowly drove" with "Civility") as he ferries the speaker to her final "House," which is the grave.

NOTICE HOW THE POEM ENDS WITH THE REVELATION THAT THIS ALL HAPPENED A LONG, LONG TIME AGO.

"Tell all the Truth but tell it slant – "
Emily resists revealing which truth she's writing about in this poem, but she claims truth is best taken in a roundabout manner ("Success in Circuit lies") rather than in one "superb surprise;" otherwise, it's too overwhelming.

NOTICE HOW SHE CONNECTS TRUTH WITH LIGHT ("LIGHTNING"), MAKING THIS POEM ABOUT ALL TYPES OF ENLIGHTENMENT.

"I'm Nobody! Who are you?"
This playful poem embraces the idea of the speaker—and the reader—being a nobody, perhaps meaning private, humble, or shy. Those aren't necessarily bad things.

NOTICE HOW THE OPPOSITE OF BEING A NOBODY—BEING A SOMEBODY—SEEMS LESS APPEALING BY COMPARISON.

"I dwell in Possibility – "
This poem is a metaphor about how the house of Possibility (writing poetry) is "superior" to the

house of Prose (writing fiction, nonfiction, or even poetry without formal qualities like rhyme or meter).

"A Thought went up my mind today – "
At the heart of this poem is the experience of déjà vu or recalling a half-remembered dream that might've been real.

PART 3: FAITH & IMAGINATION

"I never saw a Moor – "
While this speaker hasn't traveled much, they have a clear idea of what distant things look like (heather on the moor, or waves on the sea).

"The Murmur of a Bee"
The speaker is captivated by the noise of a bee, though they can't quite say why.

"If I can stop one Heart from breaking"
This poem suggests that if the speaker can help others, their life will have meaning.

"These are the days when Birds come back – "
Despite the blue skies and bright golden sun, the idea of summer returning is a "fraud."

"There's a certain Slant of light,"
A specific angle of winter sunlight prompts the speaker to contemplate issues of religion ("Cathedral Tunes") and death, which lead to divine pain that doesn't leave a mark ("find no scar").

"God gave a Loaf to every Bird – "
This poem argues that happiness is more than the accumulation of food or possessions.

"The Daisy follows soft the Sun – "
Here the sun is personified ("his golden walk") as the object of the daisy's attention.

NOTICE THAT WHILE THE LAST LINE HINTS AT EAGERNESS AND EXCITEMENT, THERE WILL ALWAYS BE DISTANCE BETWEEN THE DAISY AND THE SUN.

To Learn More About Emily Dickinson:

1   *Becoming Emily: The Life of Emily Dickinson* by Krystyna Poray Goddu. Chicago Review Press, 2019.

2   *Emily Writes: Emily Dickinson and Her Poetic Beginnings* by Jane Yolen. Henry Holt & Co., 2020.

3   *On Wings of Words: The Extraordinary Life of Emily Dickinson* by Jennifer Berne. Chronicle, 2020.

Bibliography

1   *The Complete Poems of Emily Dickinson*. Edited by Thomas H. Johnson. Little, Brown & Company, 1961.

2   Emily Dickinson Archive. https://www.edickinson.org/

3   Poetry Foundation. https://www.poetryfoundation.org/poets/emily-dickinson